With a phoenix's fire, she ignites,

An enchanting aura alights,

In the air, her magic takes flight,

She's a guiding star, shining bright.

Welcome to
Black Venuses
Self affirmation
coloring book for black women!

Embark on a colorful journey of self-expression and empowerment with this coloring book designed for women. Unleash creativity while embracing inspiring quotes that celebrate your strength and uniqueness.

Let the vibrant pages ignite your spirit!

Traveler:

_____

Color test page

The journey awaits...

I am strong and resilient.

I give and receive abundance.

I embody
divine
energy.

I leave a legacy of progress.

I am authentically myself.

Blessings flow to and from me.

I am
beautiful
inside and
out.

I inspire all those around me.

I embrace my uniqueness.

I attract abundance and positive energy.

I shape my destiny with purpose.

I spread positivity and light.

I seize every opportunity.

I am a role
model
for all.

I bloom with grace.

I'm proud of
my identity.

Grace and elegance define me.

I love and care for myself.

I ignite positive change.

I immerse in what brings me joy.

Setbacks fuel my success.

I trust my intuition.

Resilience defines me.

I am loved.

I shape my destiny.

I'm a brave
warrior.

I uplift and encourage.

I am a
lifelong
learner.

I exude confidence and grace.

I defy stereotypes effortlessly.

I am a deserving queen.

I am
beautiful
and wise.

I walk with divine purpose.

I seize every opportunity.

I reach for my dreams.

Confidence
is my
armor.

Happiness is
my
birthright.

I radiate divine energy and light.

I honor every step of my journey.

I take
initiative with
my
intelligence.

I prioritize self-care.

I draw wisdom from my ancestors.

Success is
my destiny.

I sparkle like the stars.

I lead with purpose.

I radiate joy and laughter.

Challenges are my stepping stones.

I uplift my community.

I am a deserving queen.

I am an
evolving
masterpiece.

Made in the USA
Monee, IL
12 October 2024

67710939R00063